Who Was
Daniel Boone?

T0006086

by Sydelle Kramer

illustrated by George Ulrich

Penguin Workshop

For Quinten, my own little explorer—GU

PENGUIN WORKSHOP
An imprint of Penguin Random House LLC, New York

First published in the United States of America by Penguin Workshop,
an imprint of Penguin Random House LLC, New York, 2006

Visit us online at penguinrandomhouse.com.

Library of Congress Control Number: 2005030155

Printed in the United States of America

ISBN 9780448439020   35 34 33 32 31

Contents

Who Was
Daniel Boone?

Go back in time more than two hundred years. Much of America was wilderness. Elk and bear roamed the forests, and buffalo wandered the plains. White settlers clashed with great Indian tribes. Two hundred years ago, the American frontier was wild and dangerous—people struggled just to survive.

One man, more than anyone, loved this untamed land. By foot and on horseback, he blazed trails for others to follow. A great hunter and woodsman, he led the first pioneers across the Appalachian Mountains into a paradise of fields and forests. Today we know it as the state of Kentucky. No wonder he became famous throughout the world as a frontier hero. No wonder his nickname was the Great Pathfinder.

Who was he?

Daniel Boone.

Chapter 1
The Boy Hunter

On October 22, 1734, when Daniel Boone was born, there was no United States. Back then there were thirteen colonies that all belonged to England. The Boones lived in the colony of Pennsylvania.

The Boone Family

Like many settlers in the area, the Boones were Quakers. They shared the land peacefully with Indians of different tribes. Rolling hills, green valleys, and rich black earth made it the perfect place for a boy like Daniel to grow up.

He was the sixth child of a farmer named Squire and his wife, Sarah. (The Boones had twelve children altogether.) Daniel fell in love with the outdoors almost as soon as he could walk. He hated to be inside. It was the woods that felt like his true home.

Daniel would do almost anything to avoid being cooped up in the family's log cabin—even risk his life. When he was about five, smallpox

struck the area. It was a deadly disease. The Boone children were forbidden to leave the house. It was the only way their parents could make sure they didn't catch smallpox. Daniel was miserable. He decided it would be better to get sick. That way, once he was well again, he'd be allowed out. (Once you've had smallpox, you can't catch it again.)

He and his sister hatched a plan. One night, after their parents went to sleep, the two snuck out. They headed straight to the house of a little boy who had smallpox. They wanted to make sure they got sick. So they crawled into bed with him. Then they ran home. Sure enough, both little Boones fell ill. They were lucky, though. They survived.

Daniel was tough and scrappy. If something bad happened, he always bounced back. Though he was small for his age, he was hardy and very strong. By age five, he could chop firewood with an ax as big as he was.

Daniel also had a fierce independent streak. He liked being alone. Although he had many friends, he stayed somewhat apart. His parents soon saw how stubborn he could be. Like many men of the day, Squire punished his children with a beating. He'd strike a naughty child with a rod until the child asked for forgiveness. But Daniel refused to say he was sorry. The beating would go on and on until Squire simply gave up.

In 1744, when Daniel was ten, Squire bought a big grassy field six miles from home. His cows would graze there. For the next five summers, Daniel's job was to care for the herd. Each day as the sun rose, he took the cows to the pasture. Each day as the sun set, he brought them back. Those

were perfect months for the boy: He spent all his time outside.

When Daniel wasn't guarding the herd, he went hunting. With a spear carved from a tree, he went through the fields hunting birds and other small game. His eye was sharp, his instincts keen, and he had no fear. Soon he could find animal tracks that older hunters had missed.

Daniel learned a lot about the land on his own. But not everything.

Perhaps his most important teachers were

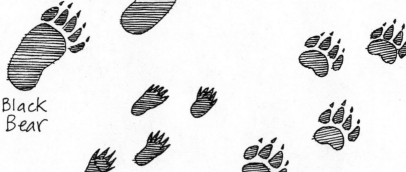

Deer

Black Bear

Raccoon

Wolf

Indians, especially the Delaware. The Delaware tribe was friendly with the Quakers. Hunting with braves—the young men in a tribe—taught the youngster tracking and trapping skills. The braves also showed him ways to survive in the forest—how to stay warm in the snow, how best to cook fresh meat. Daniel learned the ways of the Indians— to respect all of the natural world. Soon he set aside the black clothes Quakers wore. He dressed in buckskin and grew his hair like a brave. He wanted to be a man of the woods.

When Daniel was about thirteen, Squire bought him a long rifle. With such power in his hands, Daniel became an even better hunter. Now he could bring down larger game, such as deer and wild turkey. He became the best shot in the family.

Teenage Daniel was considered old enough to hunt and trap on his own. So during the fall and winter, he'd go off alone for a few days. He'd rise at dawn, when the grass was still wet with dew, and roam the forest all day. He even went hunting by moonlight. He did not kill for sport or for pleasure—he killed to have food, to stay alive. There were no grocery stores, no clothing stores. Animal skins were made into clothing, blankets, and rugs, so people could survive the cold winters. The teenager's hunting skill meant his family would never starve or freeze.

The Boone family came to rely on Daniel more and more. So did other folks. It was the custom of the time to share meat and skins with others who didn't have them. Daniel was always generous to people in need.

deer

fox

beaver

He grew to be a strong, broad-shouldered young man with piercing blue-gray eyes. Although he was known throughout Pennsylvania for sharpshooting, he had many other skills. From Squire, Daniel learned how to fix broken guns. His father also taught him to shoe horses and to repair tools and wagons. He also knew enough carpentry to build a house.

With all the work around the farm, Daniel had no time for school. He probably never set foot inside a classroom. His father, for one, didn't care.

"Let the girls do the spelling," Squire once said. "Dan will do the shooting."

When he was about fourteen, Daniel learned to read and write. The wife of one of his older brothers taught him how. He never mastered spelling, but he became a devoted reader. He took books with him on hunting trips. At night, he read by the light of the campfire. He also learned some arithmetic. Daniel's lack of schooling didn't make him different from his friends. In fact, on the frontier, he was considered well educated.

But his best subject was the woods. There, no sound escaped him, and every animal track was familiar. He rarely got lost. It was as though the trees themselves helped him find his way.

When Daniel was hunting, nothing seemed to distract him. Yet with other tasks, his mind wandered. Out in the meadow, for instance, he'd sometimes forget to watch the herd. Once, he left the cows alone for days.

It happened the summer before he turned fifteen. The herd was peacefully grazing. All of a sudden Daniel spotted fresh tracks in the pasture. A bear! Without thinking, off he went. Not only did he leave the cows, he didn't tell anyone where he was going.

By nightfall, Sarah was worried. Where was Daniel? When he still wasn't home the next morning, she became frantic. Hurrying to town, she set up a search party to find her favorite child. For two days the men looked everywhere. It seemed like Daniel had simply disappeared. His family feared he was lost in the mountains forever.

But that afternoon someone spied smoke in the distance. Was the boy alive? By evening, the men found him. Daniel was sitting happily by a fire, eating dinner. He had killed his first bear.

Now, not even sixteen years old, he was about to set out for a new frontier.

Chapter 2
Moving On

By 1750, Squire had had enough of Pennsylvania. This was partly due to his falling-out with the Quakers. Two of the Boone children had married outside the faith. According to other Quakers, they were sinners.

But there was another reason Squire wanted to leave. The area was getting too crowded. More and more settlers were moving in. That was bad for the land. Few people knew how to fertilize farmland or rotate crops. (Today these methods help farmers protect the richness of the soil.) So Squire decided to sell his property and move farther south. That's where there was plenty of cheap, fertile land.

Come April, the Boones stuffed their belongings inside a covered wagon. They set off for the colony

of Virginia. There was no road, just a rough trail. As the best woodsman in the family, Daniel was the guide. Though only fifteen years old, he led them about fifteen miles a day. Sometime in May, they reached a place near Winchester, Virginia. They had traveled nearly five hundred miles. The family stayed there for about a year. All except Daniel.

He was allowed to go on a "long hunt." That was an Indian term for a hunting trip that lasted all fall and part of winter. Once a year, for the rest of his life, Daniel would go on a long hunt. This first one took him to the Yadkin Valley in western North Carolina. The game was plentiful. The earth was rich and red, and the meadows looked perfect for grazing.

The Yadkin Valley was an ideal place for a new farm. So in 1751, Squire moved the Boones there.

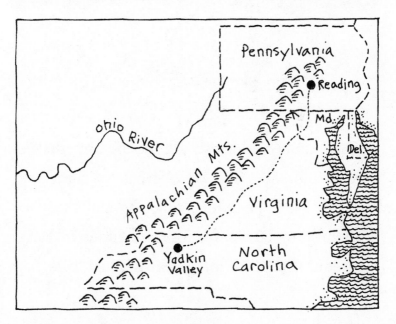

With winter coming, he and his boys quickly built a cabin. They made plans for spring planting. They were ready for the long winter.

But Daniel couldn't sit still. Besides, the Boones needed money. Off Daniel went to hunt and trap. In 1752, he sold enough animal skins for the family to buy nearly thirteen hundred acres. Soon his three-foot-long Pennsylvania rifle had a nickname. One settler claimed Daniel was so sharp a shot, he could shoot a tick off a bear's nose three hundred feet away. So Daniel started calling his rifle "Ticklicker."

The Yadkin Valley was wild country. There were few settlers around, and no towns. Much of the land was covered by forest. Before they could plant corn and wheat, the Boones had to chop down trees. They pulled out stumps and carted off boulders. It was hard work. Daniel was a willing helper. But he knew that farming was not the life for him. Where was the adventure in plowing a field? What

excitement was there in reaping and sowing? Often Daniel hoped for rain so he wouldn't have to work in the fields. Then he could head where he truly belonged—the woods.

The long hunt kept him busy in fall and winter. With the game he killed, he helped feed and clothe his family. In addition, he made money selling beaver and otter skins.

Daniel wasn't just a good hunter. He was also a famous sharpshooter. Confident, sometimes sassy, 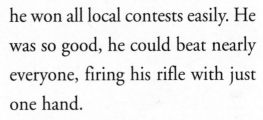 he won all local contests easily. He was so good, he could beat nearly everyone, firing his rifle with just one hand.

Then in 1753, something took his mind off the great outdoors. At a wedding, he met a black haired young woman. She was almost as tall as he was. Rebecca Bryan was the daughter of wealthy neighbors. Fifteen years old to Daniel's nineteen, she had a strong independent streak, too. The two were naturally shy, but they liked each other right away. Rebecca reminded Daniel of his mother, Sarah.

They began to spend time together. Flashing deep-brown eyes, Rebecca seemed fearless yet patient and calm. Daniel fell in love with her. But marriage had to wait. War was brewing.

In the 1700s, England and France were the two most powerful countries in Europe. They were locked in a struggle to control North America.

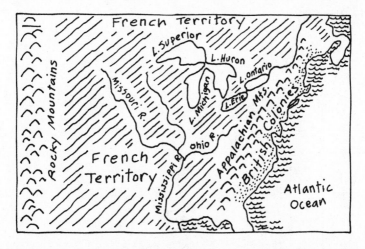

England had its thirteen colonies; the French had claimed Canada and land from the Appalachian Mountains west to the Rockies and north to the Great Lakes. War finally broke out in 1754.

Many different tribes of Indians were caught in the middle. They were losing their land to white settlers. The Indians had lived in North America for centuries. They resented pioneers like the Boones, who flocked to territory that had always been theirs.

Most of the Indian tribes ended up siding with the French in the war. They fought against the British soldiers and the British colonists. In the colonies, the war was known as the French and Indian War.

THE FRENCH AND INDIAN WAR

DESPITE A DISASTROUS BEGINNING, THE BRITISH WON THE WAR, AND CONTROL OF ALMOST ALL OF NORTH AMERICA, IN 1763. BUT THE COLONISTS WON SOMETHING, TOO—THE MAKINGS OF A NEW IDENTITY. THE WAR SHOWED THAT PEOPLE FROM ALL OVER THE COLONIES HAD SOMETHING IN COMMON: BEING AMERICAN.

BY 1776, OLD ALLIANCES HAD FLIPPED. AFTER THE COLONISTS DECLARED INDEPENDENCE, THE FRENCH HELPED THE THIRTEEN COLONIES WHILE MOST TRIBES FOUGHT WITH THE BRITISH.

Quakers do not believe in war. Nonetheless, twenty-year-old Daniel joined the British army. He felt that his family's land had to be protected. He served as a blacksmith and a supply-wagon driver. The army was under the command of a British general, Edward Braddock. The army was fifteen hundred strong. Its mission was to capture a French-held fort in Pennsylvania. Daniel was proud to be part of such a powerful army. How could it possibly lose?

However, General Braddock knew nothing about the American frontier. Nor did he understand how Indians fought. The general insisted that his troops dress in bright blue or red uniforms. He told them to attack the enemy in long, straight lines. After all, this was the way battles were fought and won in Europe. So his men marched in the open toward the fort.

But hundreds of French soldiers, Canadians, and Indian warriors lay in wait. Some crouched behind trees, while others kneeled in tall grass. They were all but invisible. Braddock and his troops were easy to spot in their blue and red coats. The French and Indians ambushed them at close range.

Even so, the British soldiers stayed in their lines. The Americans, however, scattered and hid in the woods. That way they had a chance against the enemy. But the general ordered them out. Three hours later, 977 soldiers, including General Braddock, were dead or wounded. They were "dropping like leaves in autumn," one officer said. The dead were scalped. The wagons were looted. Prisoners were taken to the fort and killed. Braddock's great army was destroyed by a force half its size.

Daniel, just a wagon driver, did not take part in the battle. From a distance, he watched the slaughter in horror. When the enemy drew near, he had to flee. Quickly he cut his team of horses loose and jumped on a horse's back. He was lucky. He rode away to safety. But he long remembered the sight of so many dead. Sad and shaken, he "had very little of the war spirit," someone who knew him wrote.

One good thing did come from his time in the army. He met a hunter named John Findley. Findley told him about a wild and glorious land. It lay west of the Appalachian Mountains. The

Iroquois Indians called it *Kanta-ke*. It was their word for "meadows." Today we know this land as Kentucky. Findley amazed Daniel with stories of valleys where corn grew as easily as grass. The forests were filled with black bear, elk, wild turkey, and deer. Buffalo roamed the plains, and flocks of geese filled the sky. It was a place with no people.

To Daniel, Kentucky sounded like paradise. He left the army. And home he went, dreaming of this new land. He had a sense that he belonged there. But Kentucky would have to wait. There were other things Daniel had to do first. He didn't want to go to Kentucky all alone. He wanted a family.

Chapter 3
The Wanderer

Daniel returned to North Carolina, and Rebecca. In 1756, he married his "little girl," as he called her. He was all of twenty-one. She was seventeen.

They had a big wedding—two other couples were married at the same time. Soon they had their own farm, and Daniel built a log house. They had no money; the cabin had only a dirt floor. Still, it was home. One year later, their first child, James, was born. Nine more children followed.

The family was a happy one. But Rebecca soon realized that her husband missed the woods. She also knew he could make more money hunting than farming. She and Daniel had a difficult decision to make. Should Daniel stick to farming and stay with his family? Or should he hunt?

They both knew that game was hard to find close to home. There were too many settlers moving into the valley. To spot deer or elk, Daniel would travel great distances. He would be away for months at a time. This meant Rebecca would raise the children and run the farm on her own. If she ran into trouble, no one would be around to help. The nearest town was far away. Meanwhile, Daniel himself would be in constant danger. If he fell ill, or had an accident, or was waylaid by Indians, that would be the end of him. Rebecca might never know what had happened to her husband.

But they realized there was no choice. Daniel was eager to go. And Rebecca was not afraid to be alone. They both understood, no matter where they lived, that they would often be apart. Indeed, Daniel ended up being away so much, he missed the births of many of his children. While Rebecca had close family and good friends, she had only a part-time husband.

In Rebecca's day, a woman made all of her family's clothing. She prepared every meal. When she wasn't cooking or sewing, spinning or weaving, she fetched water from the well or stream, chopped wood for the fire, churned butter, molded candles, cleaned the house, tended the garden, fed and cared for the livestock, planted and reaped the fields, cared for the children, and tended to the sick. Plus she had to be an excellent shot. Who else would hunt if her husband was gone?

WHAT DANIEL WORE

TO SURVIVE IN AMERICA'S FORESTS, DANIEL HAD TO CHOOSE WHAT HE WORE CAREFULLY. APPEARANCE DIDN'T MATTER. HIS CLOTHES HAD TO KEEP HIM WARM AND DRY, AND BE EASY TO MOVE AROUND IN AND HARD TO TEAR. SO HE WORE:

- A LONG, LOOSE DEERSKIN SHIRT THAT FELL TO MID-THIGH
- A LEATHER BELT THAT HELD THE SHIRT CLOSED
- A BREECHCLOUT—A CLOTH ABOUT THREE FEET LONG WRAPPED AROUND HIS LEGS LIKE PANTS
- DEERSKIN MOCCASINS, TO WALK IN NEAR-SILENCE

FROM HIS BELT HE HUNG A KNIFE, A TOMAHAWK, AND AN ANIMAL HORN THAT KEPT HIS GUNPOWDER DRY. HE ALSO CARRIED DEERSKIN POUCHES WITH HIM FOR FOOD AND SUPPLIES.

blanket
roll

tomahawk

Powder
horn

buckskin
tunic

hunting
Knife

rifle

bullet
pouch

moccasins

For his part, Daniel adored his wife and children. He missed them terribly when he was away. But he couldn't be happy living any other life. Besides, in his time, a good hunter was an honored leader in his community.

Off he went through the deepest woods. Daniel looked every inch a frontiersman now. He dressed in a combination of cloth and animal skins that kept him warm and dry. He wore moccasins, not shoes. And he never ever wore a coonskin cap.

People couldn't help but notice him. Though Daniel was of average height, he was so strong and athletic that he seemed taller. He had the rugged, fearless look of a pioneer, with a high forehead, prominent cheekbones, and a long nose. His skin was fair and his hair brown. Because his mouth was large, with thin lips, the Indians called him "wide mouth."

Daniel often traveled alone, with just his dog and horse for company. On long hunting trips,

he built himself a lean-to at every stop. A lean-to
is a shelter with three sides and an opening at the

front. Inside, he spread leaves or branches on the
ground for a bed. Right outside, he made a blazing
fire to cook elk's liver or wild turkey, his favorite
meals. The fire also warmed and lit the lean-to.
After dinner, he would stretch out under a blanket
with a book—usually the Bible, a history book, or

Gulliver's Travels by Jonathan Swift. Off came his sweaty moccasins. He'd set them near the flames to

dry. The fire also kept his feet toasty. (He believed this was the reason he stayed in good health.) His gun was always by his side, in case of attack.

Chapter 4
Still Wandering

The French and Indian War was not yet over. So there were times Daniel had to go back into the army and fight. The Cherokee were attacking settlements close to the Boones' home in North Carolina. The raids frightened Rebecca. That's why, in 1760, the Boones moved back to Virginia. They stayed there for two years, until the Cherokee in their area were defeated.

By the time the Boones returned to North Carolina, game was harder to find than ever. Daniel fell into debt. In 1764, the French and Indian War was over, but Daniel could hardly celebrate. He had to sell his land to pay his bills.

In the next few years, taxes rose. Businessmen bought up huge tracts of land to sell in little pieces for high prices. Most of the game fled or was killed. How would the Boones survive?

Daniel was frantic to find good hunting. In 1765, he thought he had the answer: Florida. Back then, Florida was wide-open territory. It was not a colony, but it was under British control. So

Daniel trekked down there with friends. What he found was a land of swamps and insects. It was so different from his mountains and woods that he

got lost. Daniel had to be rescued by Indians.

Rebecca understood that Florida was no place for the Boones. So Daniel kept on searching for the right spot. He moved the family three times in two years.

In the fall of 1767, he traveled west for a few weeks on a long hunt. Suddenly before him were mountains nearly four thousand feet high, and forests thick with magnificent trees. He'd never seen so many animals or smelled such wonderful pine. The mountains ended in plains. He hunted his first buffalo there. What was this paradise called? Kentucky, the land he'd heard about and dreamed of.

There was only one problem. Where were the meadows, the rich soil, that John Findley had described? A farm needed clear, fertile land. Daniel headed back to Rebecca loaded down with animal skins. But he feared Kentucky would never be his home.

Then his old
friend John Findley
came for a visit. Daniel
told him about his disappointing
trip. Findley listened. It turned out that Daniel
had been in the wrong place. He hadn't gone deep
enough into Kentucky. All the good farmland was
north and west.

Findley told him about the Great Warrior's
Path. It was an old and poorly marked Indian
pass. Findley said it was a "secret door" through

Kentucky's high mountains. It led west to meadows of bluegrass. Few white men had ever taken this trail.

An unknown trail! Daniel was thrilled. He was confident now that he could find the Great Warrior's Path. Indians might try to keep him from it. But he was happy to take the risk. It didn't bother him that he'd be in Indian territory. He didn't think of himself as wanting to steal what belonged to others. His idea  was simple—there was good land, and he wanted some of it. Once Rebecca agreed to the trip, there was no stopping him.

In May of 1769, he, Findley, and four other men set out. One was Rebecca's brother, John. They had fifteen horses loaded with equipment. Sure enough, they found the Great Warrior's Path. It went through the Cumberland Gap. The Cumberland Gap was a narrow notch right through the Appalachian Mountains. Gradually the peaks became rolling hills, then flat plains. Soon there were meadows of bluegrass—ideal farmland. The journey took about five weeks. In all that time, they had seen no sign of Indians.

The group split up to go hunting. Daniel headed off with his brother-in-law. Over the next few months, the two shot many deer, elk, bear, and wild turkey.

There were so many passenger pigeons, they clouded over the sky. Buffalo were so plentiful, the men feared they'd be caught in a stampede.

The buffalo had stomped out trails, called traces, right through the woods. Daniel and his brother-in-law followed the traces to hunt. They killed buffalo mainly for their tasty meat and tongues, and the delicious marrow from their bones. Also, their hides made warm clothing, blankets, and tents. Daniel and John couldn't take buffalo skins back home to sell, though. Each hide weighed close to 125 pounds—too heavy to lug back over the mountains.

Findley had been right: Kentucky was paradise in every way. Anyone could prosper. Daniel made up his mind: The Boones would move here, along with all their relatives. He was thirty-five years old now, but he'd finally found home. By the end of December, Daniel and John had a hoard of fur skins to take east and sell. But then one cold night, Daniel had a dream. It was about Squire, who had been dead four years. Daniel watched his father walk toward him but refuse to shake his hand. Daniel woke with a start. The dream was an omen. He feared that something bad was about to happen.

And it did. A band of Shawnee Indians found Daniel and John. There beside them were all the animal skins they'd collected. To the Shawnee, the two men were thieves. The king of England had

recently signed a treaty with the Shawnee. He had promised that settlers would not move beyond the Appalachians. Clearly, that promise meant nothing. These white men were trespassing on Shawnee hunting grounds.

The Shawnee took Daniel's and John's animal skins, rifles, and horses. For seven days Daniel and John were held captive.

When they were released, the braves gave them moccasins, a deerskin, a little gun, and some gunpowder. With these, they could survive in the mountains and hunt for food. The chief issued a warning: "Now, brothers, go home and stay there . . . for this is the Indians' hunting ground. . . . And if you are so foolish as to venture here again, you may be sure the wasps and yellow jackets will sting you severely."

THE SHAWNEE

THE SHAWNEE ORIGINALLY LIVED IN WHAT WE NOW CALL OHIO. BY THE TIME DANIEL CAME TO KNOW THEM, THEY HAD BEEN LABELED WARLIKE, YET HAD BEEN CONSTANTLY FORCED BY SETTLERS TO GIVE UP THEIR LAND. ONLY ABOUT FIFTEEN HUNDRED IN NUMBER, THEY HAD TO MOVE FARTHER AND FARTHER WEST, FIRST TO INDIANA, THEN TO MISSOURI AND KANSAS. FINALLY THEY CAME TO OKLAHOMA, WHERE MUCH OF WHAT IS LEFT OF THE TRIBE STILL LIVES.

TECUMSEH WAS THE SHAWNEE'S BEST-KNOWN CHIEF. HE LIVED AROUND THE SAME TIME AS DANIEL. HE FIERCELY OPPOSED GIVING UP TRIBAL LANDS AND TRIED TO LEAD INDIANS OF ALL TRIBES IN THE FIGHT TO HOLD ONTO THEM.

Tecumseh

Later Daniel said that the chief acted "in the most friendly manner." But at the time, Daniel was furious. Stubborn as ever, Daniel decided that he and his brother-in-law John would stay on Indian land and make up for their losses.

All through the winter, the two lived in a cave and hunted and trapped. The Shawnee hadn't spotted them. But one cold day John went out to check his beaver traps. He never returned. Five years later, his skeleton was found. He had probably been killed by Indians.

Losing John must have been very hard for Daniel. Now he was all alone. The Indians nearby were his enemies. Nevertheless, Daniel remained. Hunting and trapping beaver on his own, he roamed through Kentucky. He got to know the territory very well. For company he talked to himself and sang to his three dogs. He said later that he "never enjoyed himself better in his life."

He'd been away almost two years before he turned home. He was almost there when a band of Cherokee surprised him. Once again Daniel's furs and skins were taken. And when he finally arrived at his house, he was sorely disappointed. No one was there. Rebecca was at a party. It had been so long since he'd seen her, Daniel couldn't wait a moment longer. So off he went to the party. Stepping before his wife, he asked her to dance.

She took one look at the stranger before her, his clothes filthy, his beard and long hair a mess, and refused.

Then Rebecca paused to take a closer look at the man. When he spoke, his voice was familiar. "You need not refuse," he said, "for you have danced many a time with me." And he laughed.

Rebecca flung her arms around him and began to cry. Daniel was back.

Chapter 5
Paradise At Last

Word about Kentucky spread fast. Daniel had plans for a settlement there. But shady businessmen started to buy up all the land. Daniel realized he had better move quickly. He had to get back to Kentucky and claim some land. Otherwise, all of it would be gone. Rebecca agreed to sell the North Carolina farm. By September 1773, the Boones and five other families were ready to leave.

Still, it was not easy to go. Daniel's mother, Sarah, was now elderly. She was too old to move. Daniel understood that if he left, he'd never see her again.

Then there were the Indians. According to the treaty, Kentucky was off-limits. But Daniel felt that if he built a home and grew crops, the land would be his, no matter what the treaty said.

Kentucky was his chance for a bright future. He had to go.

Daniel's parting with his mother was painful. As one neighbor said, "They threw their arms

around each other's necks and tears flowed freely from all eyes." Then Daniel was gone.

Out of the Yadkin Valley Daniel went. His group included about fifty pioneers. The families had packed their belongings on horses. The path was wide enough for only one horse at a time. To keep safe, little children and chickens rode in baskets hooked to the saddles. Cattle and hogs were herded along. Despite the great danger of an Indian attack, the group had to proceed slowly.

They hadn't even reached the Cumberland Gap when Daniel realized something. Their pace was so slow, they'd soon run out of food. So he sent a group of men back to get more supplies. Among them was his sixteen-year-old son, James.

One night, as James and the men made camp, wolves began to howl. It was another bad omen. Sure enough, Indians attacked around dawn. In the eyes of the braves, James

and the others were breaking the treaty. They were stealing Indian land. No mercy was shown. James was shot and stabbed to death. Only two men escaped. They snuck back to Daniel and the others.

Daniel was grief-stricken when he heard the news. So was Rebecca. Sending his son off was a decision Daniel regretted for the rest of his life. But he was determined not to change his plans. The other pioneers, though, were too frightened to go on. They headed back to the Yadkin Valley. That left the Boones alone and without a home. They were forced to spend the winter in western Virginia, in the cabin of a friend.

But by 1774, Kentucky was legally open to white settlement. A powerful man named Richard Henderson bought up two hundred thousand acres of land. Henderson offered Daniel a deal. Daniel would build a road to Henderson's land. Then he would guide a group of settlers there and help them construct a town. When all this was accomplished, Henderson would give Daniel two thousand acres. Daniel agreed to the deal.

Henderson had bought his land from Cherokee Indians. He'd convinced them to sell it for a few thousand dollars worth of clothing, knives, guns, and liquor. However, not all the braves were happy about the sale. The young warriors of the tribe believed it would lead to disaster. White men would end up taking *all* their land from them. Dragging Canoe, the son of a famous chief, was especially furious. He told Daniel, "You have bought a fair land, but there is a cloud hanging over it. You will find its settlement dark and chilling."

Daniel ignored him. He was desperate to return to his hunter's paradise and claim his own land. In March 1775, he led another party of about thirty men out of Tennessee to the Great Warrior's Path. There was snow in the mountains and mud in the valleys. But that didn't stop them from starting a road. Chopping down trees and hacking away bushes, they widened the Path. Now wagons could cross it. Over cold, icy peaks, through rain-soaked

valleys, they built log bridges and leveled the trail. The route they created was named the Wilderness Road.

The crew trusted Daniel. He "was . . . our pilot and conductor through the wilderness," as one man said. Each day he marked the trail for them, left them to clear it, and went off to hunt for that night's meal. West of the mountains, he left the old trail behind and followed the path the buffalo took to the plains.

By April, the group had reached the heart of Kentucky. The Wilderness Road made it possible for pioneers to settle farther west than ever before. In the following years, over three hundred thousand people traveled the road to get to Kentucky and beyond. Daniel's knowledge of the woods and his fearless explorer's eye made it happen. No wonder he was known as the Great Pathfinder.

Once in Kentucky, the first order of business was to build a fort. The spot Daniel chose was near the Kentucky River. He believed its raging waters and high bank would protect the settlers from Indian attack. After the fort was built, there could be a real settlement. But as trees were chopped down and land cleared, Daniel did not fool himself about the great dangers to come. He knew the tribes would not give up this paradise easily.

The fort took shape slowly. It took three years to complete. It was designed to be about as long

as a city block. Inside its log walls were cabins for shelter. There were blockhouses where lookouts stood watch, ready to fire weapons. Storerooms called magazines held ammunition. Everyone in the group was to live inside the fort for the first year. But people were eager to claim their own land, plant crops, and start houses. They spread out over the land.

Kentucky was now their home. The group named their new settlement after the man in charge. It was called Boonesborough.

In June, Daniel returned to his family. By September, he had taken them over his new road to Kentucky. He was almost forty-one years old now. At last it seemed as though his dream had come true.

Chapter 6
Kidnapped!

Daniel built the Boones' new cabin himself. A wood floor and glass windows gave it the feel of a real house. Windows with glass were not a common sight in the wilderness. It was difficult to carry glass over the miles of mountain roads.

But while the house was comfortable, the surroundings were rough. Boonesborough was a lonely place. Most of the settlers in Kentucky were young men without families. There were only a handful of women. Rebecca had few friends. There wasn't anyone to share her fears with.

Shawnee Chief   Cherokee Chief

Boonesborough was also dangerous. The Cherokee and Shawnee had decided to join forces against the settlement. "Better to die like men than dwindle away by inches," one Shawnee chief explained. Boonesborough could be attacked at any time. There were only eighty settlers to defend it. Some of them were children.

One sleepy Sunday afternoon in the summer of 1776, the Indians pounced. Shawnee and Cherokee warriors sneaked up on the fort. They kidnapped three girls canoeing on the Kentucky River. One of them was Daniel's thirteen-year-old daughter, Jemima.

Daniel was napping when he heard an uproar outside. He leaped from his bed and raced barefoot from the house. Learning the news, he instantly took off after the Indians. He knew there was not

a minute to lose. He did not even go back for his moccasins. Other men from the settlement joined in the search. They had to get the girls before the braves returned to their village. Otherwise, there would be too many Indians to fight. The girls would be gone forever.

Jemima was a spunky teenager and close to her father. From him she had learned the ways of the frontier. She comforted her friends. She explained that the Shawnee believed it was wrong to hurt female captives. They had been kidnapped, but they would not be killed. Jemima was confident her father would come after them. But how would he know where to look?

Jemima had a plan. She and the girls left behind a trail of broken branches and pulled-up vines. Clever Jemima even tore off small bits of her skirt and left them on the ground.

For two days, Daniel and his men searched for the girls. Even though the other men could find

no trace
of them in
the dense forest,
Daniel picked up
the trail. He spotted
the little signs Jemima had left.
Sure enough, on the third day, Daniel saw
smoke ahead. They were catching up!

The braves' camp was just ahead. Through the trees Daniel could see four Indians making a fire and preparing a meal. He flopped to the ground. Then he crawled toward them "on his breast like

a snake," Jemima said later. When she caught her father's eye, he signaled her to keep quiet. He was planning his own surprise attack.

Suddenly there was a rifle shot. One of the braves fell, wounded. Jemima shouted, "That's Daddy!" The girls, all weeping, broke for the woods. The Indians fled. Daniel had his daughter

back. He told his men, "Thank Almighty Providence, boys, for we have the girls safe. Let's all sit down by them now and have a hearty cry." Then he took Jemima into his arms.

But that was not the end of the danger. Far from it. The tribes and the settlers still battled over who had the right to the land. In fact, the fighting between them grew even more complicated.

It was 1776. The American colonies no longer wanted to belong to England. They longed to be a free country—the United States. The American Revolution broke out. Now the British and Americans were enemies. The British encouraged the Indians to attack the colonists. There were rewards for each American scalp. In turn, the settlers' hatred and fear of the Indians grew. Even the Indians who wanted peace were murdered.

Daniel didn't think much about the American Revolution. This may sound surprising for a frontier hero. But not all colonists wanted war. To Daniel, the Revolution was a distant war. Battles were fought on American soil far from where the Boones lived.

Daniel's fight was with the Indians.

One friend said about Daniel, "He never liked to take life and always avoided it when he could." Nevertheless, he wanted the Indians' land, both for himself and for other settlers. He helped take the wilderness away from native tribes. But unlike many settlers, he did not personally hate the Indians. His Quaker parents had taught him to respect others. As a backwoodsman, he had hunted with many braves. He had learned about the woods from them. He admired their customs and values.

Still, in 1777, Daniel led his men into battle against the Shawnee Indians. When the braves swooped down on Boonesborough, it was Daniel who cried, "Boys, we have to fight!" He personally led the charge. In the end, the Indians retreated, but Daniel was shot in the

ankle. The bullet broke the bone. It took months for his foot to heal.

Boonesborough survived its first big test, and all because of Daniel. He was a natural leader. Though shy and sometimes distant, he had a calm manner that inspired trust. Never one to boast, he was quiet, even-tempered, and honest. People respected his decency and his know-how. They believed in him.

Now Daniel and Boonesborough were about to face their greatest challenge.

Chapter 7
The Siege

By January of 1778, there was hardly any food in Boonesborough. All that remained was meat. But the settlers were almost out of salt, and without salt, the meat would go bad. Soon they'd all be starving.

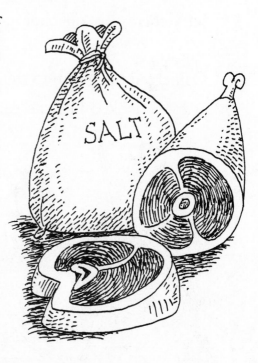

Daniel had an idea that might save them. But it was risky. He knew there were salt springs at the nearby Licking River. If a group camped there, they could use kettles to boil down the water and scrape out the salt. Twenty-four men would have to go. The process would take weeks. Boonesborough would be left unprotected. The Indians might attack again.

Still, there was no choice. They had to find salt.

Daniel led the group to the river. As the weeks went by, it looked like the gamble had paid off.

There would be plenty of salt to take back to Boonesborough.

Then one snowy February day, Daniel went hunting for buffalo to feed the crew. Suddenly, out of nowhere, four Shawnee appeared. In a flash, Daniel took off. He raced through the snow.

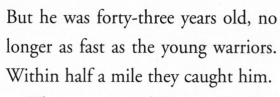

But he was forty-three years old, no longer as fast as the young warriors. Within half a mile they caught him.

There was nothing to do but surrender. To show he was giving up, he leaned his rifle against a tree. Daniel Boone, the great frontiersman, was now a prisoner of the Shawnee.

They didn't kill him. Instead they walked him three miles to their camp. Their great chief, Blackfish, was there. So were one hundred and twenty warriors in full war paint. Daniel had no idea what was going to happen next.

The chief had a plan. He knew Daniel was Boonesborough's leader. What if Daniel joined the tribe? If he did, the other settlers would join, too. The white men would take the place of Shawnee

warriors killed in battle. And Boonesborough
would disappear.

When Daniel heard the chief's plan, he didn't
know what to do.

What was the best way to save Boonesborough?
He was desperate. So he told the chief that he would
get the men at the Licking River to surrender. They
would join the tribe if the Shawnee promised not
to kill anyone. Then, in the spring, Daniel would
return to Boonesborough and convince the settlers
to become Shawnee, too.

Blackfish accepted. At noon the next day, Daniel was marched at gunpoint out of the Shawnee camp. He led the warriors to his friends at the river. The white men, spotting the Indians, ran for their guns. Daniel shouted to them, "Don't fire. If you do, all will be massacred." On his advice, they all surrendered.

Some Shawnee braves, however, still wanted to kill the captives. The white men had always broken their word. So what did it matter if the braves broke theirs?

Daniel spoke before the Shawnee. In an emotional voice, he said that he and his friends were good hunters: They could help the tribe.

Blackfish let the braves vote on the fate of the white men. A painted wooden club was handed from brave to brave. If a man passed it on, he was voting for mercy. But if he threw it to the ground, he was voting for death. Daniel watched closely. His life and the lives of his friends were on the line.

One by one the braves cast their vote. All one hundred and twenty of them. The vote was very close. It was 61-59 to spare the men. But Daniel had to pay a price for the vote of mercy. The Shawnee made him run the gauntlet.

The gauntlet was an Indian test of courage. It was also a form of punishment. The braves formed two lines, facing each other. Daniel had to run between the lines as the braves beat him with sticks and clubs. The only way to escape death was to run at top speed. If he fell, he was doomed. Daniel was not as young or as fast as he used to be. The braves had caught him once before. Could he make it through the gauntlet?

Later, he said, "I set out full speed, first running so near one line that they could not do me much damage," then he ran close to the other line of men. Over and over, the braves struck him with their weapons. But still Daniel kept moving. At last he could see the end of the line.

Suddenly a warrior stepped into his path. He was blocking Daniel to keep him from finishing. But Daniel bent forward—he ran right at the man's chest. *Whomp!* He knocked the brave flat on his back.

Daniel made it to the end of the line! Everyone—even the Indians—cheered. They gathered around to shake his hand. Now Daniel would become an honorary brave.

In the Shawnee village, the women, or squaws, took him to the river. Believing that a bath could wash away the whiteness in his soul, they scrubbed him clean. Then they plucked out all the hair on his head, except for a forelock. He looked just like a Shawnee warrior. The tribe gave him an Indian name—Sheltowee, or Big Turtle. Blackfish adopted him: Daniel was now his son.

Time passed, and Daniel's white friends began to distrust him. They were prisoners of the Shawnee. They were not treated the same way Daniel was. Had they been captured because he'd betrayed them? Some thought so. Whispers of "traitor" started behind Daniel's back.

Daniel didn't care what the men thought. His concern was saving Boonesborough. He knew the Shawnee were planning to surround it. His family was in danger. So were all the settlers. He had to find a way to warn them and help them fight off attack.

But how could he escape? Though he was an honorary brave, the Shawnee didn't trust him. They watched his every move. Four months passed with no chance to slip away. Then one day outside the village, some wild turkey appeared. The braves went off to hunt them. Daniel knew it was now or never. He grabbed a horse and galloped off.

It was 160 miles to Boonesborough. Would he get there in time? He rode the horse so fast and hard, it died. So he continued on foot, covering his trail so the Shawnee couldn't catch him. He

zigzagged across forests, splashed down streams, even swam the great Ohio River. He didn't even stop to eat.

Four days later, Daniel stumbled into Boonesborough and rushed to the family cabin.

It was empty.

Where had Rebecca and the children gone? He sank down on a chair, in despair. Suddenly the family cat appeared and leaped into his lap. Was the animal all that was left of his family?

What had happened?

Somehow rumors had spread all the way to Boonesborough. Rumors that Daniel was a traitor. The settlers lost faith in him. Rebecca no longer felt comfortable in the place Daniel had founded. She had taken the children and moved back to North Carolina.

Daniel was alone and friendless. But he was not going to let Boonesborough be destroyed. He gathered the settlers together and told them the Shawnee were planning to attack. He said he was home to help his people fight. Although the group did not welcome him, they listened. And they believed him.

Boonesborough got to work under Daniel's command. Extra food was brought in. The women made new bullets and bandages. More people arrived to help defend the settlement. But Daniel knew they were still at a great disadvantage. There were only fifty men inside the fort, plus women and children. Blackfish would arrive with an army of four hundred.

It was early September when the Shawnee rode up to the fort at Boonesborough. Blackfish called for Big Turtle. Daniel strode out to meet him. The two sat on a blanket and talked. The chief hoped that Daniel would keep his word and convince the settlement to surrender.

When Daniel returned to the fort, he told the settlers what Blackfish wanted. The settlers talked for a long time. Theirs was a difficult choice. In the end they all agreed. They would not surrender to the Shawnee. They would fight. Even though many of them might die.

Daniel didn't tell Blackfish that. The longer the delay, the more ready Boonesborough would be to fight. So he told the chief that the settlers needed more time to make a decision.

The next day, there was surprising news. Blackfish made another offer. The Shawnee would sign a peace treaty. But in return the whites had to stop crossing the Ohio River. They also had to join the side of the British in the Revolution.

The settlers pretended to agree. The two sides held a feast outside the fort. Men on both sides smoked a peace pipe and shook hands.

Then shots suddenly rang out. No one knew who fired them. Daniel and the settlers quickly returned to the fort. Soon angry warriors surrounded it. The siege of Boonesborough had begun.

The next day there was constant shooting from both sides. Inside the fort, families were terrified. Horses and cattle stampeded in panic.

The Shawnee tried to set the fort on fire with burning arrows. But Daniel knew that fire was not the biggest threat. Outside, the braves were digging a tunnel. Their plan was to tunnel inside the fort. If they succeeded, they would easily destroy Boonesborough.

A week passed. The tunneling never stopped. Each night, blazing arrows flamed across the sky. The settlers used so much water to put out fires that the fort's supply ran low. There hadn't been much food before, but now all the fruit and vegetables had been eaten. If the siege continued much longer, everyone would starve to death.

On the eleventh night, the Shawnee turned up their firepower. The walls of Ft. Boonesborough were in flames. This was it—the decisive battle.

Suddenly rain began to fall. Soon it was pouring. And it didn't stop. The rain went on for hours. It snuffed out the blaze and, even better, created mud. The mud made the Indians' tunnel collapse. When the sun rose the next day, all was silent outside. The Shawnee were gone.

Boonesborough was saved!

DANIEL'S COURT-MARTIAL

AFTER THE SIEGE OF BOONESBOROUGH ENDED, DANIEL WAS CHARGED BY TWO SETTLERS WITH TREASON. THERE WAS A COURT-MARTIAL, WHICH IS A MILITARY TRIAL. THEY HEARD TESTIMONY THAT DANIEL HAD BETRAYED HIS FRIENDS TO THE INDIANS AND SUPPORTED THE BRITISH IN THE AMERICAN REVOLUTION. DANIEL SPOKE IN HIS OWN DEFENSE AND EXPLAINED HIS ACTIONS.

THE VERDICT CAME QUICKLY. DANIEL WAS FOUND NOT GUILTY. STILL, IT WAS A SHAMEFUL EVENT FOR HIM. DANIEL NEVER TALKED ABOUT THE TRIAL. IN FACT, HIS YOUNGEST SON AND SOME OF HIS GRANDCHILDREN KNEW NOTHING OF IT.

Chapter 8
A New Home

Daniel left for North Carolina to be reunited with his family. Rebecca told him she was reluctant to return to Kentucky. The strife with the Indians had worn her down. She was fearful of more attacks. And she knew the people of Boonesborough were no longer their friends.

But Daniel couldn't imagine living anywhere but Kentucky. Besides, he was owed two thousand acres of land for building Boonesborough. It made sense to go back.

That's what the Boones did, in 1779. But they didn't return to their old cabin. They didn't want to live among people who distrusted their family. So he and Rebecca founded Boone's Station, six miles away.

Unfortunately, life was no more peaceful there than in Boonesborough. The next years were hard ones. Daniel lost his claim to the land Henderson had promised him. He found himself fighting the Shawnee again. His brother Edward was scalped by Shawnee braves. His son Israel died before his eyes. Where was the paradise he had dreamed of when he'd crossed the mountains all those years ago?

In 1783, the American Revolution ended. The colonists won. A new nation was born—the United States of America. In Kentucky, the major Indian

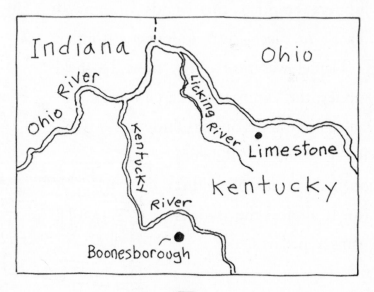

wars also ended. As the defeated tribes moved farther west, thousands of whites began streaming into the territory. They followed along Daniel's Wilderness Road. The wealthy bought up land and sold it at high prices. Daniel watched poor pioneer families like his lose what they thought was theirs, just as the Indians once had.

It was a bitter feeling. He had opened this land to whites, yet he himself owned none of it. Indeed, he was penniless. Worse, his beloved Kentucky wilderness was disappearing. White hunters emptied the woods of animals. This place—*his* place—was no longer a frontier.

Daniel was nearly fifty now. To make money, the family moved to a town called Limestone, on the Ohio River. There, Rebecca opened a tavern. She didn't run it alone—the Boones had seven slaves.

Today, all Americans see that slavery—owning human beings—was a horrible crime. But in Daniel's time, there were many people who accepted or approved of it. They considered slaves their property. They didn't think of them as human beings. Farmers who owned slaves saved a lot of money—slaves never got paid for their work.

Still, most Quakers were against the practice. No one knows for sure why Daniel and Rebecca accepted it. What historians do know is that in the 1700s, there were still Pennsylvania Quakers who owned slaves. Plus, slavery was common in North Carolina, Virginia, and Kentucky. So wherever Daniel and Rebecca went, they saw slaves and knew people who owned them. It did not seem wrong to them. The Boone family continued to own slaves until 1865, when the Civil War ended and did away with the terrible practice once and for all.

In Limestone, Daniel found work as a surveyor.

That meant he measured land, marking its boundaries. The work allowed him to charge high fees and finally to claim land for himself. But he wasn't very good at the job. Clients constantly sued him. They said that he hadn't measured properly. Others challenged his land claims in court. He almost always lost. He was no match for crafty businessmen and lawyers.

Daniel was in a rut, and nothing could lift him out of it—not even fame. In 1784, a book called *The Adventures of Col. Daniel Boon* made him a legend in both America and Europe. (His last name was misspelled.)

That didn't help him financially. As the years passed, his money problems got worse. When Kentucky became a state in 1792, it made no difference to his prospects. By 1796, the man who had first brought settlers there decided there was only one thing for him to do: leave.

It didn't matter that he was now nearly sixty-five years old. Missouri, to the west, was beckoning. It was real wilderness, unlike Kentucky, which was now much more heavily settled.

So once again, in 1799, the Boones moved. Daniel and Rebecca, three sons and their wives, two daughters and their husbands, seventeen grandchildren, and assorted other relatives set out.

DANIEL AND HIS KIDNAPPERS

BY THE TIME DANIEL MOVED TO MISSOURI, THE SHAWNEE WERE LIVING THERE AS WELL. HE VISITED THEIR VILLAGE OFTEN, GOING HUNTING WITH THE BRAVES. EVERY NOW AND THEN, SHAWNEE WARRIORS WOULD VISIT HIM AT HOME. AMONG THEM WERE SOME WHO HAD KIDNAPPED HIM IN 1778. DANIEL WOULD SIT WITH THE BRAVES BY A FIRE OUTSIDE HIS CABIN AND TALK ABOUT THE TIME HE'D LIVED WITH THEM AS AN ADOPTED SON. ONE BRAVE WOULD SAY, "DAN, YOU REMEMBER WHEN WE HAD YOU PRISONER?" DANIEL'S GRANDCHILDREN WOULD GATHER AROUND, AND THE STORYTELLING WOULD BEGIN.

For the trip to Missouri, they built dugout canoes and packed everything they owned tightly inside. With Daniel and his slaves driving their livestock along the river, the family paddled down the Ohio to the Mississippi. On the way, somebody called out and asked Daniel why he was leaving. "Too crowded," was his answer. "I need more elbow room."

The Boone clan arrived in St. Louis and then headed northwest of the city. In 1800, Daniel was given a large tract of land. His own land. At last he was free to hunt and roam again. His companion in the Missouri woods was a young slave who became his best friend. The great backwoodsman felt at home again.

Was this finally the end of hardship? No. Daniel mangled his hand in a steel trap. Then he nearly killed himself falling through ice on the Missouri River. He also watched three of his daughters die of disease, and lost all his land again.

But the wilderness still called to him. In his
seventies, he traveled the farthest west he'd ever
been—to Yellowstone, in Wyoming. The trip took
six months.

Then in 1813 came a blow from which he never
really recovered. Rebecca died after a short illness
at the age of seventy-four. Daniel was helpless with
grief. He sat alone in his fields for weeks, his rifle
in his arms.

DANIEL'S BEST FRIEND

DANIEL'S SON OWNED A SLAVE NAMED DERRY COBURN. HE WAS A BACKWOODSMAN ALMOST AS SKILLED AS DANIEL HIMSELF. DERRY'S WIFE AND CHILDREN WERE OWNED BY VARIOUS MEMBERS OF DANIEL'S FAMILY. IN 1801, THE TWO MEN BEGAN TO HUNT TOGETHER AND PROVED NEARLY PERFECT COMPANIONS. ONE BOONE FAMILY MEMBER SAID DERRY "WAS A MAN OF THAT SAME PECULIAR DISPOSITION WHICH CHARACTERIZED DANIEL BOONE, NON-COMMUNICATIVE." DANIEL AND DERRY SAT TOGETHER FOR HOURS WITHOUT TALKING, BUT IN TOTAL COMFORT. IT WAS AS THOUGH THEY KNEW EACH OTHER'S THOUGHTS. ON A HUNT, DANIEL WOULD SHOOT, AND DERRY WOULD COOK. HE PREPARED VENISON THE WAY DANIEL LIKED IT—WITH SPICY RED PEPPER.

Derry Coburn

For the rest of his life, he lived with one or another of his children. Sensing the end was near, Daniel had a coffin built. He insisted it be stored in his son's house. From time to time, he polished it, even lay down in it. He commented before he died that he'd "taken many a nice nap in it."

Death finally took Daniel on

September 26, 1820. He was eighty-five. His last words were, "I'm going. My time has come."

Chapter 9
The Great Pathfinder

Few Americans have loved the wilderness as deeply as Daniel Boone. The most famous backwoodsman of his time, he never truly settled down. Most of his life was spent hunting or exploring. No other white person knew the land as well as Daniel. He could find a path through any forest, track any animal, outlast the worst weather. Despite almost constant danger, he used his skill and daring to open Kentucky to pioneers. And beyond that, the wide West. The new United States grew and prospered thanks, in part, to him.

In Daniel's time, settling the frontier meant taking land away from the first Americans—the Indians. Thousands died fighting over it, Indians and settlers alike. Though he respected and learned much from Indians, Daniel thought he had just as much right to the land as they did. He also owned slaves, yet his close companion, Derry, was a slave owned by Daniel's son. It may be difficult to understand, but Daniel's world was very different from ours. So were his ideas of what was right and wrong. Still, to this day Daniel stands as America's first frontier hero, and its most important pioneer. The Great Pathfinder helped the United States grow and become the country it is today.

DANIEL BOONE
Born: 1734
Died: 1820

TIMELINE OF DANIEL'S LIFE

1734	Daniel is born in Pennsylvania.
1750	Daniel and his family move to Virginia; Daniel goes on his first "long hunt."
1750	Daniel serves with the British in the French and Indian War.
1751	The Boones move to the Yadkin River valley of North Carolina.
1756	Daniel marries Rebecca Bryan.
1757	Daniel and Rebecca's first child, James, is born.
1765	Daniel goes exploring in Florida.
1767	Daniel reaches Kentucky.
1769	Daniel goes back to Kentucky to hunt.
1773	Daniel tries to take his family to Kentucky, but his son James is killed by Indians. They turn back.
1775	Daniel carves the Wilderness Road out of the forest and founds Boonesborough.
1776	Daniel rescues his daughter from Shawnee braves.
1778	The Shawnee capture Daniel; the chief Blackfish adopts Daniel as son; settlers withstand the siege of Booneborough.
1784	Daniel is made famous by the book *The Adventures of Col. Daniel Boon.*
1798	A Kentucky county is named for Daniel, but most of his land is sold to pay taxes.
1799	Daniel moves to Missouri.
1813	Rebecca dies at the age of seventy-four.
1820	Daniel dies at the age of eighty-five.

TIMELINE OF THE WORLD

The Danish explorer Vitus Bering discovers Alaska. — 1741

Benjamin Franklin invents the lightning rod. — 1752

The French and Indian War begins. — 1754

The French and Indian War ends. — 1763

James Watt invents the steam engine. — 1769

The Boston Tea party dumps tea in Boston Harbor, — 1773
protesting the British tea tax.

The Continental Congress meets in Philadelphia. — 1774

The Declaration of Independence is signed. — 1776

James Cook discovers Hawaii. — 1778

Britain recognizes the U.S. as an independent nation. — 1783

George Washington is inaugurated the first American president. — 1789

Kentucky becomes a state. — 1792

John Adams is elected America's second president. — 1796

The U.S. makes the Louisiana Purchase; Robert Fulton — 1803
invents the steamboat.

Abraham Lincoln is born. — 1809

The U.S. and Britain fight the War of 1812. — 1812

The U.S. defeats Britain, ending the War of 1812. — 1815

Construction of the Erie Canal begins. — 1817

The U.S. and Canada agree on their border. — 1818

The U.S. buys Florida from Spain. — 1819

The Missouri Compromise allows slavery in Missouri and — 1820
everywhere south of Missouri to the Rockies.

BIBLIOGRAPHY

Aron, Stephen. **How the West Was Lost.** Johns Hopkins University Press, Baltimore, 1999.

Draper, Lyman C., edited with an Introduction by Ted Franklin Belue. **The Life of Daniel Boone.** Stackpole, Mechanicsburg, 1998.

Faragher, John Mack. **Daniel Boone: The Life and Legend of an American Pioneer.** Henry Holt, New York, 1992.

Hargrove, Jim. **Daniel Boone.** Children's Press, Chicago, 1985.

McCarthy, Pat. **Daniel Boone: Frontier Legend.** Enslow Publishers, Berkeley Heights, 2000.

Streissguth, Tom. **Daniel Boone.** Carolrhoda, Minneapolis, 2002.